Bleuette's

Book of Days

and

other important stuff

by

Pamela Wolf

This book belongs to

_____

| Sunday | Monday | Tuesday | Wednesday | Thursday | Friday | Saturday |
|--------|--------|---------|-----------|----------|--------|----------|
|        |        |         |           |          |        |          |
|        |        |         |           |          |        |          |
|        |        |         |           |          |        |          |
|        |        |         |           |          |        |          |
|        |        |         |           |          |        |          |

Did you know that the first 20,000 Bleuette dolls were given away free to the first subscribers to La Semaine de Suzette?

# January_____

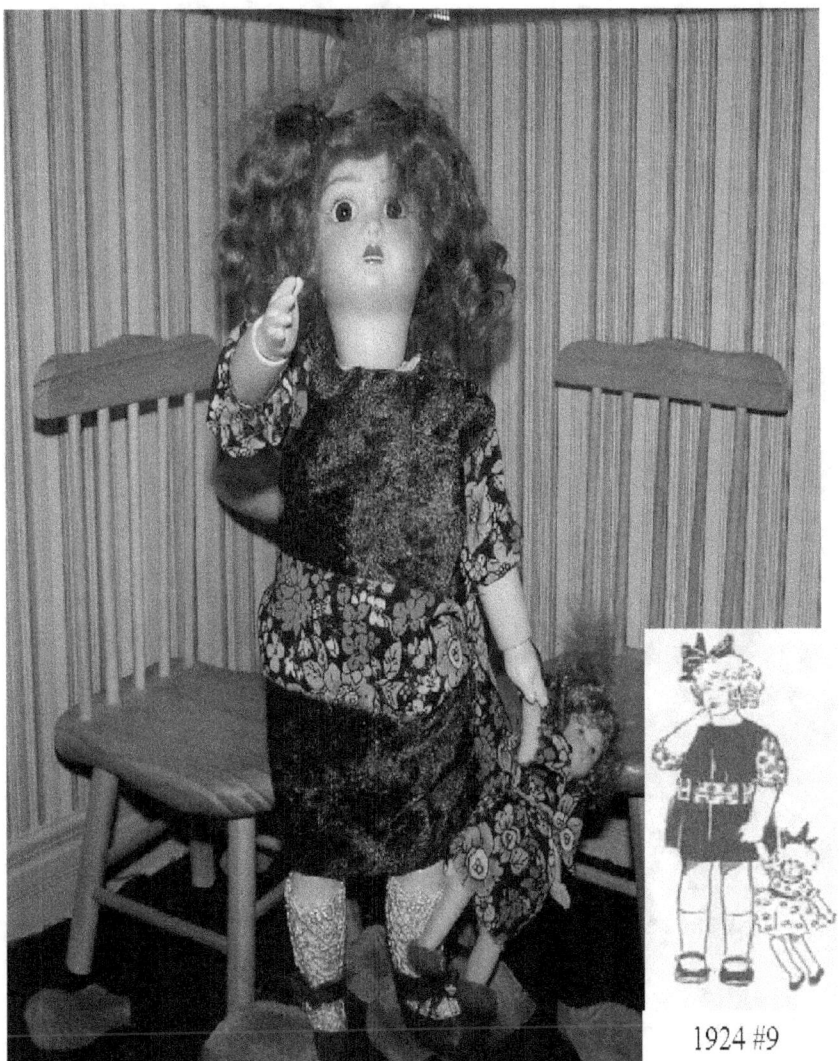

1924 #9

Octavia is wearing 1924#9 notice the similarity
of her picture to the LSDS illustration.

Octavia and Timothy at the 10<sup>th</sup> anniversary Bleuette sewing Club Gala.

Week of _____

| Day/Date | Appointments |
|----------|--------------|
| Sunday | |
| Monday | |
| Tuesday | |
| Wednesday | |
| Thursday | |
| Friday | |
| Saturday | |

Octavia had a good time at the ball and came home without Timothy.

Week of _____

| Day/Date | Appointments |
|----------|--------------|
| Sunday | |
| Monday | |
| Tuesday | |
| Wednesday | |
| Thursday | |
| Friday | |
| Saturday | |

Timothy came home with another girl in a red dress.
He wouldn't say who it was. None of the other girls
would tell me anything either.

Week of _____

| Day/Date | Appointments |
|----------|--------------|
| Sunday | |
| Monday | |
| Tuesday | |
| Wednesday | |
| Thursday | |
| Friday | |
| Saturday | |

Timothy also likes driving his fire truck.
He shows off for one of the other girls.

Week of _____

| Day/Date | Appointments |
|----------|--------------|
| Sunday | |
| Monday | |
| Tuesday | |
| Wednesday | |
| Thursday | |
| Friday | |
| Saturday | |

You've heard the rhyme Peter, Peter pumpkin
eater had a wife and couldn't keep her?

Week of _____

| Day/Date | Appointments |
|---|---|
| Sunday | |
| Monday | |
| Tuesday | |
| Wednesday | |
| Thursday | |
| Friday | |
| Saturday | |

| Sunday | Monday | Tuesday | Wednesday | Thursday | Friday | Saturday |
|--------|--------|---------|-----------|----------|--------|----------|
|        |        |         |           |          |        |          |
|        |        |         |           |          |        |          |
|        |        |         |           |          |        |          |
|        |        |         |           |          |        |          |
|        |        |         |           |          |        |          |

The first issue of La Semaine de Suzette was February 2 1905. Don't forget to mark this special day for Bleuette's birthday.

# February_____

Omia and Ondrea made the perfect valentine.

They made a list of what they
wanted on their valentine.

Week of _____

| Day/Date | Appointments |
|---|---|
| Sunday | |
| Monday | |
| Tuesday | |
| Wednesday | |
| Thursday | |
| Friday | |
| Saturday | |

Omia asked me to draw a heart
then write the message
"I'll be bleu if you won't be mine."

Week of _____

| Day/Date | Appointments |
|---|---|
| Sunday | |
| Monday | |
| Tuesday | |
| Wednesday | |
| Thursday | |
| Friday | |
| Saturday | |

Ondrea picked the little drummer for the graphic. She said it reminded her of a beating heart full of love.

Week of _____

| Day/Date | Appointments |
|----------|--------------|
| Sunday | |
| Monday | |
| Tuesday | |
| Wednesday | |
| Thursday | |
| Friday | |
| Saturday | |

They make sure that everything is right
before it gets printed out.

Week of _____

| Day/Date | Appointments |
|---|---|
| Sunday | |
| Monday | |
| Tuesday | |
| Wednesday | |
| Thursday | |
| Friday | |
| Saturday | |

| Sunday | Monday | Tuesday | Wednesday | Thursday | Friday | Saturday |
|--------|--------|---------|-----------|----------|--------|----------|
|        |        |         |           |          |        |          |
|        |        |         |           |          |        |          |
|        |        |         |           |          |        |          |
|        |        |         |           |          |        |          |
|        |        |         |           |          |        |          |

Did you know that between the years of 1941 and 1946 during the second world war that LSDS was not published because France was occupied by Germany?

# March_____

Orabel waits by the fire for the leprechauns to
come and bring her a pot of gold on St. Patrick's Day.

Orabel wears a ladybug dress in the bathroom of the dollhouse
that has also been invaded by ladybugs!

Week of _____

| Day/Date | Appointments |
|----------|--------------|
| Sunday | |
| Monday | |
| Tuesday | |
| Wednesday | |
| Thursday | |
| Friday | |
| Saturday | |

Orabel and Opal Lou model Les Alveolus a
dress from the 1950's.

# Week of _____

| Day/Date | Appointments |
|---|---|
| Sunday | |
| Monday | |
| Tuesday | |
| Wednesday | |
| Thursday | |
| Friday | |
| Saturday | |

Orabel studies with her sisters using her laptop.
Looks like she is not doing her lessons!

Week of _____

| Day/Date | Appointments |
|---|---|
| Sunday | |
| Monday | |
| Tuesday | |
| Wednesday | |
| Thursday | |
| Friday | |
| Saturday | |

Orabel is teaching Octavia to have bad study
habits they are looking at the Bleuette Sewing club site again
when they should be studying.

# Week of _____

| Day/Date | Appointments |
|---|---|
| Sunday | |
| Monday | |
| Tuesday | |
| Wednesday | |
| Thursday | |
| Friday | |
| Saturday | |

Rose and Orabel join hands on the porch  in their
new dresses when Rose came for a visit.

# Week of _____

| Day/Date | Appointments |
|----------|--------------|
| Sunday | |
| Monday | |
| Tuesday | |
| Wednesday | |
| Thursday | |
| Friday | |
| Saturday | |

| Sunday | Monday | Tuesday | Wednesday | Thursday | Friday | Saturday |
|--------|--------|---------|-----------|----------|--------|----------|
|        |        |         |           |          |        |          |
|        |        |         |           |          |        |          |
|        |        |         |           |          |        |          |
|        |        |         |           |          |        |          |
|        |        |         |           |          |        |          |

LSDS always came out on Thursday. The last issue published was
25 August 1960.

# April____

Omia models Alba, a dress from G-L from the 1930's.

Frippon come back, that street is full of cars!
You might get run over!

Week of _____

| Day/Date | Appointments |
|---|---|
| Sunday | |
| Monday | |
| Tuesday | |
| Wednesday | |
| Thursday | |
| Friday | |
| Saturday | |

What a good dog you are Frippon.
You do such a good job of sitting

Week of _____

| Day/Date | Appointments |
|---|---|
| Sunday | |
| Monday | |
| Tuesday | |
| Wednesday | |
| Thursday | |
| Friday | |
| Saturday | |

Omia models her dress and shoes for the great
Teal challenge near the fountain .

Week of _____

| Day/Date | Appointments |
| --- | --- |
| Sunday | |
| Monday | |
| Tuesday | |
| Wednesday | |
| Thursday | |
| Friday | |
| Saturday | |

Olea is Omia's twin, she is modeling a dress made
from vintage fabric with a hanky that is used as
the bodice. The scalloped edges made all the hems.

Week of _____

| Day/Date | Appointments |
|----------|--------------|
| Sunday | |
| Monday | |
| Tuesday | |
| Wednesday | |
| Thursday | |
| Friday | |
| Saturday | |

Olea models Petite Carreaux, a dress from
G-L from the 1930's.

Week of _____

| Day/Date | Appointments |
|----------|--------------|
| Sunday | |
| Monday | |
| Tuesday | |
| Wednesday | |
| Thursday | |
| Friday | |
| Saturday | |

| Sunday | Monday | Tuesday | Wednesday | Thursday | Friday | Saturday |
|--------|--------|---------|-----------|----------|--------|----------|
|        |        |         |           |          |        |          |
|        |        |         |           |          |        |          |
|        |        |         |           |          |        |          |
|        |        |         |           |          |        |          |
|        |        |         |           |          |        |          |

In 1930 and 1931 Bleuette
had a lot of patterns for sports and costumes from all nations.
Her favorite sport was tennis,
she has a number of tennis outfits both in
patterns  and G-L outfits.

# May _____

Oleandra says hello to the girls when she
comes to the house.

It's a lot of fun to play in the blue
bonnets in the field.

# Week of _____

| Day/Date | Appointments |
|----------|--------------|
| Sunday | |
| Monday | |
| Tuesday | |
| Wednesday | |
| Thursday | |
| Friday | |
| Saturday | |

Frippon finds a critter in the trash can!

Week of _____

| Day/Date | Appointments |
|----------|--------------|
| Sunday | |
| Monday | |
| Tuesday | |
| Wednesday | |
| Thursday | |
| Friday | |
| Saturday | |

Papillon knocked over the flower pot and
is scolded by Olicia.

Week of _____

| Day/Date | Appointments |
|---|---|
| Sunday | |
| Monday | |
| Tuesday | |
| Wednesday | |
| Thursday | |
| Friday | |
| Saturday | |

Omia wears a reproduction of maman's wedding dress.

Week of _____

| Day/Date | Appointments |
|---|---|
| Sunday | |
| Monday | |
| Tuesday | |
| Wednesday | |
| Thursday | |
| Friday | |
| Saturday | |

Little Red Riding Hood meets the wolf
on the way to grandma's house. This is my interpretation of one of
the G-L outfits.

Week of _____

| Day/Date | Appointments |
|---|---|
| Sunday | |
| Monday | |
| Tuesday | |
| Wednesday | |
| Thursday | |
| Friday | |
| Saturday | |

| Sunday | Monday | Tuesday | Wednesday | Thursday | Friday | Saturday |
|--------|--------|---------|-----------|----------|--------|----------|
|        |        |         |           |          |        |          |
|        |        |         |           |          |        |          |
|        |        |         |           |          |        |          |
|        |        |         |           |          |        |          |
|        |        |         |           |          |        |          |

Bleuette has more than 1060
patterns available in her magazine spanning six decades.

June _____

The big bambinos play with an
antique toy tractor.

Dolls from the 2007 Bleuette
Retreat in Kansas City.

Week of _____

| Day/Date | Appointments |
|----------|--------------|
| Sunday | |
| Monday | |
| Tuesday | |
| Wednesday | |
| Thursday | |
| Friday | |
| Saturday | |

I called this one wishful thinking.
Trudy and Olicia are trying to beat the heat
by thinking of a snowman.

Week of _____

| Day/Date | Appointments |
|----------|--------------|
| Sunday | |
| Monday | |
| Tuesday | |
| Wednesday | |
| Thursday | |
| Friday | |
| Saturday | |

Goose helps Oberta water the plants in her
new dress called chevron.

Week of _____

| Day/Date | Appointments |
|----------|--------------|
| Sunday | |
| Monday | |
| Tuesday | |
| Wednesday | |
| Thursday | |
| Friday | |
| Saturday | |

The girls had fun making some of the craft projects
from the LSDS pages.

Week of _____

| Day/Date | Appointments |
| --- | --- |
| Sunday | |
| Monday | |
| Tuesday | |
| Wednesday | |
| Thursday | |
| Friday | |
| Saturday | |

Osmi show off her skating skill in some recycled
skates from two mismatched pairs.

Week of _____

| Day/Date | Appointments |
|----------|--------------|
| Sunday | |
| Monday | |
| Tuesday | |
| Wednesday | |
| Thursday | |
| Friday | |
| Saturday | |

| Sunday | Monday | Tuesday | Wednesday | Thursday | Friday | Saturday |
|--------|--------|---------|-----------|----------|--------|----------|
|        |        |         |           |          |        |          |
|        |        |         |           |          |        |          |
|        |        |         |           |          |        |          |
|        |        |         |           |          |        |          |
|        |        |         |           |          |        |          |

Over the years the doll was given a younger sister, Benjamine, in 1926, which was on the market only a short time, then a baby brother, Bambino in 1928. An older sister, Rosette, was her companion in her last years between 1955 and 1960.

# July _____

Daisy Odette is going to spend her summer days going fishing.
Looks like she already caught one for her supper!

Othello a bambino reproduction found a good
way to beat the summer heat.

Week of _____

| Day/Date | Appointments |
|----------|--------------|
| Sunday | |
| Monday | |
| Tuesday | |
| Wednesday | |
| Thursday | |
| Friday | |
| Saturday | |

Oxana a Recknagel doll and the boys
cool off on the porch.

Week of _____

| Day/Date | Appointments |
|---|---|
| Sunday | |
| Monday | |
| Tuesday | |
| Wednesday | |
| Thursday | |
| Friday | |
| Saturday | |

Olicia rushes to put out a fire!

Week of _____

| Day/Date | Appointments |
|---|---|
| Sunday | |
| Monday | |
| Tuesday | |
| Wednesday | |
| Thursday | |
| Friday | |
| Saturday | |

Olympia, Otalie and Opal show off their
challenge dresses for the bleuette gathering
for the UFDC convention.

Week of _____

| Day/Date | Appointments |
|----------|--------------|
| Sunday | |
| Monday | |
| Tuesday | |
| Wednesday | |
| Thursday | |
| Friday | |
| Saturday | |

Ondrea found an interesting way to open
the bottle of champagne!

# Week of _____

| Day/Date | Appointments |
| --- | --- |
| Sunday | |
| Monday | |
| Tuesday | |
| Wednesday | |
| Thursday | |
| Friday | |
| Saturday | |

| Sunday | Monday | Tuesday | Wednesday | Thursday | Friday | Saturday |
|--------|--------|---------|-----------|----------|--------|----------|
|        |        |         |           |          |        |          |
|        |        |         |           |          |        |          |
|        |        |         |           |          |        |          |
|        |        |         |           |          |        |          |
|        |        |         |           |          |        |          |

From February 1905 to April 1920patterns directions  were given by tante
Jacqueline Rivière
(pseudonym of Jeanne Bernhardt).

# August _____

Oberta models Mascot, a G-L fashion.

Octavia shows off the doll collection
that the O'girls have collected.

Week of _____

| Day/Date | Appointments |
| --- | --- |
| Sunday | |
| Monday | |
| Tuesday | |
| Wednesday | |
| Thursday | |
| Friday | |
| Saturday | |

Olicia models Greta from the 1930's

Week of _____

| Day/Date | Appointments |
|---|---|
| Sunday | |
| Monday | |
| Tuesday | |
| Wednesday | |
| Thursday | |
| Friday | |
| Saturday | |

O'hannah shows off Ping Pong from the 1930's.

Week of _____

| Day/Date | Appointments |
|---|---|
| Sunday | |
| Monday | |
| Tuesday | |
| Wednesday | |
| Thursday | |
| Friday | |
| Saturday | |

Otelia models the
presentation
dress from the 1940's.

Week of _____

| Day/Date | Appointments |
|----------|--------------|
| Sunday | |
| Monday | |
| Tuesday | |
| Wednesday | |
| Thursday | |
| Friday | |
| Saturday | |

Ondora models a solid color version of Domino

Week of _____

| Day/Date | Appointments |
|---|---|
| Sunday | |
| Monday | |
| Tuesday | |
| Wednesday | |
| Thursday | |
| Friday | |
| Saturday | |

| Sunday | Monday | Tuesday | Wednesday | Thursday | Friday | Saturday |
|--------|--------|---------|-----------|----------|--------|----------|
|        |        |         |           |          |        |          |
|        |        |         |           |          |        |          |
|        |        |         |           |          |        |          |
|        |        |         |           |          |        |          |
|        |        |         |           |          |        |          |

From June 1920 until April 1932 the patterns are signed Suzanne River, pseudonym Susan Bernhardt (daughter of "Aunt Jacqueline").

September_____

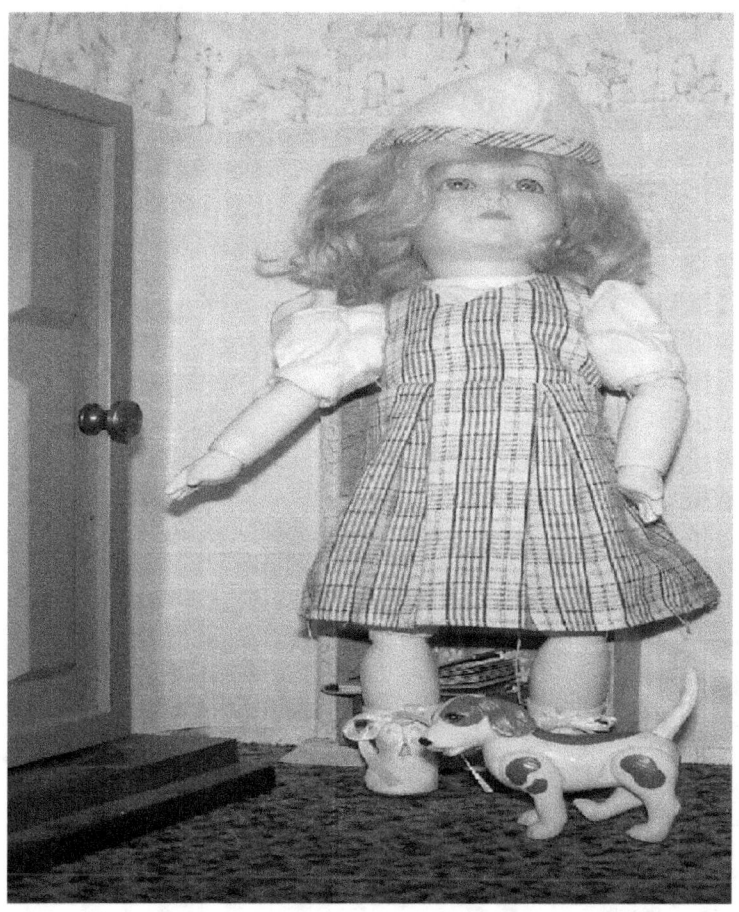

Trudy models Bon petite Diable as she goes
out the door with dog.

Okendra models a dress made from hankies for
a challenge at the Bleuette Sewing club yahoo group.

Week of _____

| Day/Date | Appointments |
| --- | --- |
| Sunday | |
| Monday | |
| Tuesday | |
| Wednesday | |
| Thursday | |
| Friday | |
| Saturday | |

Onika and Oberta show off their matching jumpers from
the plaid challenge at the Bleuette Sewing Club.

Week of _____

| Day/Date | Appointments |
|---|---|
| Sunday | |
| Monday | |
| Tuesday | |
| Wednesday | |
| Thursday | |
| Friday | |
| Saturday | |

Oneida gets help preparing for school with
the help of Mini-bleuette.

Week of _____

| Day/Date | Appointments |
|----------|--------------|
| Sunday | |
| Monday | |
| Tuesday | |
| Wednesday | |
| Thursday | |
| Friday | |
| Saturday | |

Oberon and Oberta model their dresses made from
the same fabric and pattern. The different trim gives them a
different look.

Week of _____

| Day/Date | Appointments |
|----------|--------------|
| Sunday | |
| Monday | |
| Tuesday | |
| Wednesday | |
| Thursday | |
| Friday | |
| Saturday | |

You might need a magnifying glass to check out what
kind of french Okendra was actually studying.

# Week of _____

| Day/Date | Appointments |
|---|---|
| Sunday | |
| Monday | |
| Tuesday | |
| Wednesday | |
| Thursday | |
| Friday | |
| Saturday | |

| Sunday | Monday | Tuesday | Wednesday | Thursday | Friday | Saturday |
|--------|--------|---------|-----------|----------|--------|----------|
|        |        |         |           |          |        |          |
|        |        |         |           |          |        |          |
|        |        |         |           |          |        |          |
|        |        |         |           |          |        |          |
|        |        |         |           |          |        |          |

Becassine was born in 1905 from a printer's plate created at the last moment in order to settle the first issue of the Semaine de Suzette and only reappeared later in the magazine to please the readers' requests.

# October _____

The O'Girls are having a Halloween party.
O'hannah is wearing one of Bleuette's many aprons.

Olea and Oberon enjoy the party. Olea's dress is one the LSDS patterns. Oberon's dress is Martha Nichol's simple Becassine pattern.

Week of _____

| Day/Date | Appointments |
|----------|--------------|
| Sunday | |
| Monday | |
| Tuesday | |
| Wednesday | |
| Thursday | |
| Friday | |
| Saturday | |

The girls gather at the table of goodies with
their host the scarecrow.

Week of _____

| Day/Date | Appointments |
|---|---|
| Sunday | |
| Monday | |
| Tuesday | |
| Wednesday | |
| Thursday | |
| Friday | |
| Saturday | |

Olea is popular at this party! She enjoys an
ice cream float with scarecrow.

# Week of _____

| Day/Date | Appointments |
|---|---|
| Sunday | |
| Monday | |
| Tuesday | |
| Wednesday | |
| Thursday | |
| Friday | |
| Saturday | |

Uh, oh it looks like the two Becassines decided
to make a feast of the cupcakes!

Week of _____

| Day/Date | Appointments |
|----------|-------------|
| Sunday | |
| Monday | |
| Tuesday | |
| Wednesday | |
| Thursday | |
| Friday | |
| Saturday | |

I hope this isn't what it looks like! O'hannah knows better than to give champagne to Dog.

Week of _____

| Day/Date | Appointments |
|----------|--------------|
| Sunday | |
| Monday | |
| Tuesday | |
| Wednesday | |
| Thursday | |
| Friday | |
| Saturday | |

| Sunday | Monday | Tuesday | Wednesday | Thursday | Friday | Saturday |
|--------|--------|---------|-----------|----------|--------|----------|
|        |        |         |           |          |        |          |
|        |        |         |           |          |        |          |
|        |        |         |           |          |        |          |
|        |        |         |           |          |        |          |
|        |        |         |           |          |        |          |

Bleuette had a Becassine costume in October 1908
and February 1959.
The one in 1908 was a lot more
complicated to make!

# November _____

Olympia is an Indian princess for a day.

It looks like Omia and Olea are having more fun playing in the leaves with Sparky instead of cleaning them up!

## Week of _____

| Day/Date | Appointments |
|----------|--------------|
| Sunday | |
| Monday | |
| Tuesday | |
| Wednesday | |
| Thursday | |
| Friday | |
| Saturday | |

Opal makes friends with one of the horses.

Week of _____

| Day/Date | Appointments |
|---|---|
| Sunday | |
| Monday | |
| Tuesday | |
| Wednesday | |
| Thursday | |
| Friday | |
| Saturday | |

I hope O'hannah knows this turkey is ready to cook!

Week of _____

| Day/Date | Appointments |
| --- | --- |
| Sunday | |
| Monday | |
| Tuesday | |
| Wednesday | |
| Thursday | |
| Friday | |
| Saturday | |

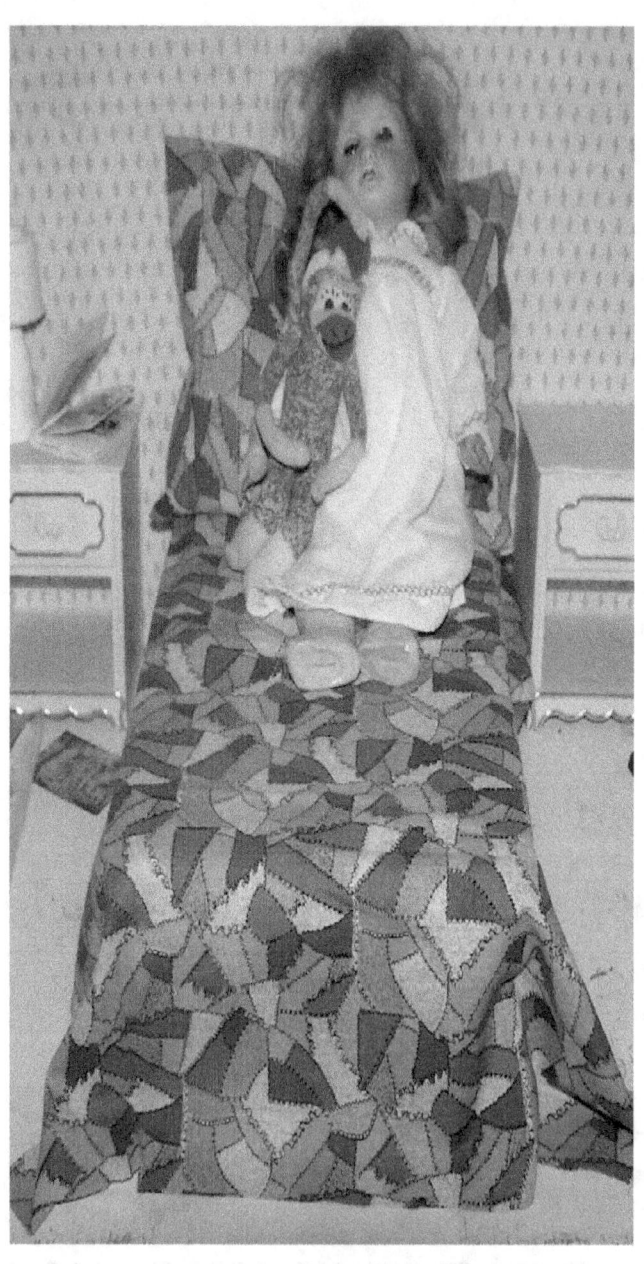

Olympia enjoys a snooze in the bedroom
on a cheater quilt.

# Week of _____

| Day/Date | Appointments |
| --- | --- |
| Sunday | |
| Monday | |
| Tuesday | |
| Wednesday | |
| Thursday | |
| Friday | |
| Saturday | |

| Sunday | Monday | Tuesday | Wednesday | Thursday | Friday | Saturday |
|--------|--------|---------|-----------|----------|--------|----------|
|        |        |         |           |          |        |          |
|        |        |         |           |          |        |          |
|        |        |         |           |          |        |          |
|        |        |         |           |          |        |          |
|        |        |         |           |          |        |          |

Did you know that not all of the patterns for Bleuette were
not all for clothes? She had crafts and furniture too!!

# December _____

Ondrea shows off her skating skill.

Omia waits for Santa

Week of _____

| Day/Date | Appointments |
|----------|--------------|
| Sunday | |
| Monday | |
| Tuesday | |
| Wednesday | |
| Thursday | |
| Friday | |
| Saturday | |

Sharing Christmas treats is much better
when you have a new sister.

## Week of _____

| Day/Date | Appointments |
|---|---|
| Sunday | |
| Monday | |
| Tuesday | |
| Wednesday | |
| Thursday | |
| Friday | |
| Saturday | |

Olea and Ondrea mail a letter to Santa while
the raccoon and Papillon watch.

# Week of _____

| Day/Date | Appointments |
|---|---|
| Sunday | |
| Monday | |
| Tuesday | |
| Wednesday | |
| Thursday | |
| Friday | |
| Saturday | |

Oberta on Christmas morning

## Week of _____

| Day/Date | Appointments |
|---|---|
| Sunday | |
| Monday | |
| Tuesday | |
| Wednesday | |
| Thursday | |
| Friday | |
| Saturday | |

Doesn't this little Bambino make
a cute Santa clause?

# Week of _____

| Day/Date | Appointments |
|---|---|
| Sunday | |
| Monday | |
| Tuesday | |
| Wednesday | |
| Thursday | |
| Friday | |
| Saturday | |

What pattern did Bleuette have the
most patterns for in the issues of
La Semaine de Suzette?

If you tell me the answer I will
give you a free book.

Important

stuff

section

Opal Lou reads a story to the animals
in the bedroom.

This is the section of the book where you record
all the important stuff like address and
birthdays and those notes that you want
to remember.

address book

Oberta shows off Trio from the 1950's. She also shows that
she is good at taking care of the little ones.

Name _____
Address _____

Phone _____
Email _____

Name _____
Address _____

Phone _____
Email _____

Name _____
Address _____

Phone _____
Email _____

Name _____
Address _____

Phone _____
Email _____

Name _____
Address _____

Phone _____
Email _____

Name _____
Address _____

Phone _____
Email _____

Name _____
Address _____

Phone _____
Email _____

Name _____
Address_____

Phone_____
Email_____

Name _____
Address_____

Phone_____
Email_____

Name _____
Address_____

Phone_____
Email_____

Name _____
Address_____

Phone_____
Email_____

Name _____
Address_____

Phone_____
Email_____

Name _____
Address_____

Phone_____
Email_____

Name _____
Address_____

Phone_____
Email_____

Name _____

Address _____

Phone _____

Email _____

Name _____

Address _____

Phone _____

Email _____

Name _____

Address _____

Phone _____

Email _____

Name _____

Address _____

Phone _____

Email _____

Name _____

Address _____

Phone _____

Email _____

Name _____

Address _____

Phone _____

Email _____

Name _____

Address _____

Phone _____

Email _____

Name _____

Address _____

Phone _____

Email _____


Name _____

Address _____

Phone _____

Email _____


Name _____

Address _____

Phone _____

Email _____


Name _____

Address _____

Phone _____

Email _____


Name _____

Address _____

Phone _____

Email _____


Name _____

Address _____

Phone _____

Email _____


Name _____

Address _____

Phone _____

Email _____

Name _____

Address _____

Phone _____

Email _____

Name _____

Address _____

Phone _____

Email _____

Name _____

Address _____

Phone _____

Email _____

Name _____

Address _____

Phone _____

Email _____

Name _____

Address _____

Phone _____

Email _____

Name _____

Address _____

Phone _____

Email _____

Name _____

Address _____

Phone _____

Email _____

Name _____
Address_____

Phone_____
Email_____

Name _____
Address_____

Phone_____
Email_____

Name _____
Address_____

Phone_____
Email_____

Name _____
Address_____

Phone_____
Email_____

Name _____
Address_____

Phone_____
Email_____

Name _____
Address_____

Phone_____
Email_____

Name _____
Address_____

Phone_____
Email_____

Name _____
Address _____

Phone _____
Email _____

Name _____
Address _____

Phone _____
Email _____

Name _____
Address _____

Phone _____
Email _____

Name _____
Address _____

Phone _____
Email _____

Name _____
Address _____

Phone _____
Email _____

Name _____
Address _____

Phone _____
Email _____

Name _____
Address _____

Phone _____
Email _____

Internet Passwords

Omette figured out my password to the internet
so now she searches the Bleu door site for new patterns!

Site name _____
User name _____
Password _____

Site name _____
User name _____
Password _____

Site name _____
User name _____
Password _____

Site name _____
User name _____
Password _____

Site name _____
User name _____
Password _____

Site name _____
User name _____
Password _____

Site name _____
User name _____
Password _____

Site name _____
User name _____
Password _____

Site name _____
User name _____
Password _____

Site name _____
User name _____
Password _____

Site name _____
User name _____
Password _____

Site name _____
User name _____
Password _____

===

Site name _____
User name _____
Password _____

===================================================

Site name _____
User name _____
Password _____

===================================================

Site name _____
User name _____
Password _____

===================================================

Site name _____
User name _____
Password _____

===================================================

Site name _____
User name _____
Password _____

===================================================

Site name _____
User name _____
Password _____

===================================================

Site name _____
User name _____
Password _____

===================================================

Site name _____
User name _____
Password _____

===================================================

Site name _____
User name _____
Password _____

===================================================

Site name _____
User name _____
Password _____

===================================================

Site name _____
User name _____
Password _____

```
================================================
Site name _____
User name _____
Password_____
================================================
Site name _____
User name _____
Password _____
================================================
Site name _____
User name _____
Password_____
================================================
Site name _____
User name_____
Password_____
================================================
Site name _____
User name _____
Password_____
================================================
Site name _____
User name_____
Password_____
================================================
Site name _____
User name_____
Password_____
================================================
Site name _____
User name_____
Password_____
================================================
Site name _____
User name _____
Password_____
================================================
Site name _____
User name_____
Password_____
================================================
Site name _____
User name _____
Password_____
```

Birthdays, Anniversaries and other important days

Oberon and Oberta bake a cake for my Birthday.

Name_____

Birthday_____

Anniversary_____

_____

_____

===================================================

Name_____

Birthday_____

Anniversary_____

_____

_____

===================================================

Name_____

Birthday_____

Anniversary_____

_____

_____

===================================================

Name_____

Birthday_____

Anniversary_____

_____

_____

===================================================

Name_____

Birthday_____

Anniversary_____

_____

_____

===================================================

Name_____

Birthday_____

Anniversary_____

_____

_____

===================================================

Name_____

Birthday_____

Anniversary_____

_____

Name_____

Birthday_____

Anniversary_____

_____

_____

============================================

Name_____

Birthday_____

Anniversary_____

_____

_____

============================================

Name_____

Birthday_____

Anniversary_____

_____

_____

============================================

Name_____

Birthday_____

Anniversary_____

_____

_____

============================================

Name_____

Birthday_____

Anniversary_____

_____

_____

============================================

Name_____

Birthday_____

Anniversary_____

_____

_____

============================================

Name_____

Birthday_____

Anniversary_____

_____

_____

Name_____

Birthday_____

Anniversary_____

_____

_____

=============================

Name_____

Birthday_____

Anniversary_____

_____

_____

=============================

Name_____

Birthday_____

Anniversary_____

_____

_____

=============================

Name_____

Birthday_____

Anniversary_____

_____

_____

=============================

Name_____

Birthday_____

Anniversary_____

_____

_____

=============================

Name_____

Birthday_____

Anniversary_____

_____

_____

=============================

Name_____

Birthday_____

Anniversary_____

_____

_____

Name_____

Birthday_____

Anniversary_____

_____

_____

===========================================

Name_____

Birthday_____

Anniversary_____

_____

_____

===========================================

Name_____

Birthday_____

Anniversary_____

_____

_____

===========================================

Name_____

Birthday_____

Anniversary_____

_____

_____

===========================================

Name_____

Birthday_____

Anniversary_____

_____

_____

===========================================

Name_____

Birthday_____

Anniversary_____

_____

_____

===========================================

Name_____

Birthday_____

Anniversary_____

_____

_____

_____

Name_____

Birthday_____

Anniversary_____

_____

_____

===============================================

Name_____

Birthday_____

Anniversary_____

_____

_____

===============================================

Name_____

Birthday_____

Anniversary_____

_____

_____

===============================================

Name_____

Birthday_____

Anniversary_____

_____

_____

===============================================

Name_____

Birthday_____

Anniversary_____

_____

_____

===============================================

Name_____

Birthday_____

Anniversary_____

_____

_____

===============================================

Name_____

Birthday_____

Anniversary_____

_____

_____

===============================================

For those other things you need to remember